SAVE YOUR LIFE,

MY WIFE DID

# Save Your Life, My Wife Did

## BY LOWERING HER A1C LEVEL BY 8 POINTS IN 8 MONTHS

Paige E. Johnson, Ph.D.

Copyright © 2019 Paige E. Johnson, PhD

ISBN:
978-621-434-085-9 (softcover)
978-621-434-087-3 (eBook)

All rights reserved. No part of this publication may be reproduced, stored in a retrieval system, or transmitted in any form or by any means - electronic, mechanical, photocopy, recording, scanning, or other – except for brief quotations in critical reviews or articles, without the prior written permission of the publisher.

Published by:

OMNIBOOK CO.
99 Wall Street, Suite 118
New York, NY 10005
USA
+1-866-216-9965
www.omnibook.org

First Edition

For e-book purchase: Kindle on Amazon, and Barnes & Noble
Book purchase: Amazon.com, Barnes & Noble,
and www.omnibook.org

Omnibook titles may be purchased in bulk for educational, business, fund-raising, or sales promotional use.
For more information please e-mail
info@omnibookcompany.com

# TABLE OF CONTENTS

| | |
|---|---|
| Introduction | 1 |
| Step One – Setting Priorities | 5 |
| Step Two – Hydration of Your Body | 11 |
| Step Three – Medications | 17 |
| Step Four – Exercise | 19 |
| Step Five – Diet Management | 25 |
| Step Six – Adequate Sleep | 37 |
| Summary | 39 |
| Conclusion | 41 |
| About the Author | 45 |

# INTRODUCTION

This is the story of my wife, Sharon, who suffered from undiagnosed diabetes and her determined struggle to manage it and save her life. This book details the process she followed (and continues to follow) to lower her A1C level from 13.8—near the highest range of 14.0—to a healthy 5.8.

My wife was diagnosed with Type II diabetes at age 51. Before turning 50, she appeared healthy. However, she began gaining weight, increasing from 140 to 245 pounds. She experienced frequent urination, extreme fatigue, severe mood swings, dry and flaky skin, fluid retention in her feet (along with numbness and tingling), reduced mental clarity, and other alarming health issues. Concerned for her well-being, I took her to the doctor. The diagnosis revealed a dangerously high A1C level of 13.8, a fasting blood sugar level of 465, and Type II diabetes, which required immediate treatment.

Here is a background leading up to Sharon's Type II diabetes diagnosis. She rarely fell ill, usually experiencing only an occasional cold, sinusitis once a year, or sometimes bronchitis. Before her diagnosis, she developed an overactive bladder, which was a minor inconvenience, and increased eye pressure. Her eye doctor started a glaucoma monitoring and prevention program, as elevated eye pressure is a symptom of glaucoma and a complication often linked to diabetes.

That year was exceptionally hot, especially in August, as expected. My wife, Sharon, struggled to tolerate the heat. Every time she stepped outside during the hottest part of the day, she felt unwell.

In August, a lightning strike near our house caused significant electrical damage. It destroyed our television and satellite system and required extensive rewiring. The repairs took about six weeks to complete, costing a lot of money and creating a great deal of frustration. Being without television during the intense August heat made the situation even more stressful. At that time, my wife and I assumed her worsening symptoms were due to stress rather than diabetes.

At the end of August, I had to travel for business, and Sharon accompanied me since I use a wheelchair and might need her assistance. During the trip, it became clear that her overactive bladder symptoms were worsening, and she was experiencing extreme thirst. Before we left, she had consulted one of her doctors, but both she and the doctor assumed her symptoms were due to the stress of a difficult summer rather than an underlying medical condition.

The trip was incredibly difficult. Sharon was constantly drinking water or rushing to the bathroom. Each morning, before or during breakfast, she drank at least two 32-ounce glasses of water. Between breakfast and lunch, she finished another 32-ounce glass. For lunch, she had a large diet soda along with yet another 32-ounce glass of water. In the afternoon, she drank another full glass before dinner.

When we went out to eat, the waiter had to bring two extra pitchers of water in addition to her original glass because she was so thirsty. After dinner and before bed, she limited herself to half a 32-ounce glass to avoid waking up too many times during the night.

Looking back, that excessive water intake may have saved her life.

When we returned home, Sharon was feeling very unwell, so she went to see her doctor. During our three-week trip, she had lost 30 pounds without understanding why. She believed it was due to all the water she had been drinking. Her doctor tested her A1C level, which came back at a dangerously high 13.8. That was when she was officially diagnosed with diabetes. The doctor immediately started her on a treatment plan to manage the condition. This included a glucometer (blood glucose meter), medications, and diabetes education. Sharon was devastated by the diagnosis and spent most of the day in tears.

Sharon met with the hospital's diabetes education nurse and a diabetes nutritionist. During her visit, the nurse used her new glucometer to check her blood sugar. It registered at a dangerously high 465—and it was not even noon yet.

What I did not know at the time was that the nurse strongly advised Sharon to go to the hospital emergency room. However, she chose not to tell me. She insisted that she felt fine, believed she did not need hospitalization, and refused to go. She did not fully understand how dangerously high her blood sugar was or the serious health risks involved. The nurse scheduled her for diabetes education sessions at the hospital.

Sharon went home and began researching diabetes and ways to lower her blood sugar. She was eager to attend the diabetes education sessions at her local hospital, hoping to learn more about managing her condition. This was the start of her journey toward reducing her blood sugar and regaining control of her health.

*Step One*

# SETTING PRIORITIES

Many people do not realize that diabetes can be deadly. It is not an acute illness but a chronic disease that progresses silently. It does not always produce obvious warning signs, yet high blood sugar slowly—and sometimes irreversibly—damages the body. Diabetes is primarily a vascular disease, but over time, it can lead to serious tissue and organ damage. If left uncontrolled, it will eventually harm some parts of the body, leading to severe complications that can be life-threatening. More often, however, diabetes causes significant disabilities before it becomes fatal. Blindness, heart disease, limb amputation, and an increased risk of cancer are all potential consequences of uncontrolled diabetes. This does not mean these complications are inevitable, but the risk is much higher if blood sugar levels are not properly managed. Maintaining healthy blood sugar levels greatly increases the chances of avoiding these serious health issues.

High blood sugar can be deadly, but more importantly, it will gradually restrict your lifestyle. Red blood cells are responsible for carrying oxygen and nutrients throughout the body. When these cells become coated with excess sugar, they struggle to deliver the necessary oxygen to vital organs. Without sufficient oxygen and nutrients, these organs begin to deteriorate or stop functioning properly.

Certain parts of the body are especially vulnerable. The retina and optic nerve in the eyes are highly sensitive to oxygen deprivation, putting vision at risk. The heart needs oxygen to pump blood effectively, and the brain—like all nerve tissue—relies on a steady oxygen supply to function properly. With diabetes, the organs are slowly suffocating, and some will fail sooner than others.

Diabetes also weakens the body's ability to heal. Cuts, abrasions, and infections take longer to recover, increasing the risk of complications. While death is inevitable for everyone, most people want to maintain a healthy, active life for as long as possible. Managing blood sugar is essential to achieving that goal.

Most of us want to see clearly, walk easily, and think sharply. However, just because you do not currently have major heart problems, vision issues, infections, or other circulatory complications does not mean you are in perfect health. If excess sugar continues to circulate in your blood, depriving your organs of oxygen and essential nutrients, serious health problems will eventually arise—it is only a matter of time. Your body was once in balance, but now it is not. It is time to reassess your priorities and take steps to restore that balance. Life is full of compromises, and over time, you may have made unhealthy choices that have taken a toll on your body. Now, you have a decision to make: choose to live. And to truly live, you must take control of your health.

The A1C test measures the percentage of your red blood cells that are coated with sugar. This number provides a clear indication of how much sugar is present in your bloodstream over time. For example, my wife's A1C was 13.8, meaning 13.8% of her blood cells were coated with sugar. An A1C of 15% or higher is considered dangerously high and can be life-threatening. In contrast, most healthy individuals have an A1C level between 2% and 6%.

Sharon had just visited her eye doctor and informed him about her diabetes and high blood sugar levels. He was deeply concerned and prescribed eye drops to help protect her vision from worsening into full-scale glaucoma and possible blindness. At this point, life had started to feel overwhelming for Sharon. She had been struggling emotionally, but the realization that diabetes could rob her of her eyesight was a turning point. She knew she had to set clear priorities for her health. Among them, preserving her eyesight was one of the most important. To do that, she had to bring her blood sugar under control—and the sooner, the better.

There is a common myth saying that you can eat whatever you want and simply adjust your medication to compensate. Many people believe that modern medicine has a pill for every problem—that a doctor can prescribe medication to make health issues disappear. This mindset is especially common among Type II diabetics, who often assume that taking medication alone is enough to control their blood sugar. While medication is essential for many, it is not a magic solution. Achieving and maintaining healthy blood sugar levels require more than just pills—it also requires lifestyle changes and other health strategies.

While medication is necessary, it can put significant strain on the liver and kidneys. The liver must break down the medication, allowing the kidneys to filter it out. This process places stress on the body and, over time, can contribute to liver damage and kidney failure. However, without medication, other vital systems may deteriorate even faster. Managing diabetes requires a careful balance, and finding the right approach should be done in close consultation with a doctor.

My wife wanted to support her body in lowering her blood sugar naturally. Through a combination of treatment and lifestyle changes, she has successfully reduced her medication dosage by more than half and has even eliminated one medication entirely. She now takes only two diabetes medications, which she will likely need for the rest of her life. However, by reducing her reliance on medication, she has significantly lessened the strain on her liver and kidneys, improving her overall health.

You must decide whether to take an active role in improving your health. Achieving and maintaining good health is a lifelong commitment, especially for those with diabetes. When I talk about health, I am not just referring to avoiding colds or the flu. I mean keeping your body functioning at its best, preserving your life, your vision, your limbs, and your ability to enjoy life for as long as possible.

Improving your health will strengthen your body's ability to fight off common illnesses like colds and the flu. If you do get sick, a healthier body will be better equipped to recover and resist infections. There are no guarantees of a long life, accidents or other non-diabetic health issues can still occur. However, the goal is to improve and maintain your health for a better quality of life. Focus on what you can do now to become healthier. Once you achieve that, you can develop strategies to stay as healthy as possible for the future.

Everyone must set their own priorities in life. When it comes to physical well-being, most people's top priority is survival. The second is usually maintaining good health, and the third is achieving financial stability. Only after these fundamental needs are met can family responsibilities and other concerns be fully addressed. Philosophical priorities, such as faith or patriotism, may come before or after physical needs. However, none of these priorities can be pursued without first being alive and healthy. Even if you feel overwhelmed by family responsibilities or work obligations, neglecting your health will eventually prevent you from fulfilling those duties. Taking care of yourself is not selfish—it is necessary. In fact, those around you, including your family and employer, should recognize that prioritizing your health benefits everyone in the long run.

Sharon decided that if she was going to live, her top priority was preserving her vision. Protecting her eyesight became her greatest focus, which meant she had to lower her blood sugar and keep it under control. She read books and pamphlets on managing blood sugar, carefully analyzing the information and creating a strategy that suited her needs. No single approach provided a complete solution, so she combined multiple strategies into six key steps. Except for Step One, which is Setting Priorities, the steps are not ranked by importance. However, each one plays a vital role in her success.

Just like a swimmer, you can swim using only your left arm or only your right arm. However, using both arms makes swimming easier, more efficient, and more effective. If you also use your legs, swimming becomes even smoother and more powerful. In the same way, you should take advantage of all the strategies available to you. My wife applied every step in her plan to improve her health. However, if certain strategies conflict with your top priorities, it is best to avoid them. If specific foods make you sick or could harm you, do not eat them. Ultimately, this is about your health and your life. The choices you make should support your well-being.

*Step Two*

# HYDRATION OF YOUR BODY

In addition to taking multiple medications, Sharon had to make significant lifestyle changes. One of the easiest changes for her to start with was increasing her water intake. Books and pamphlets recommend drinking 64 ounces of water per day. Healthy individuals should consume at least this amount, and it should be pure water, not other fluids like coffee, soda, juice, or milk. Since the human body is made up of more than 70 percent water, staying hydrated helps regulate body fluids and flush out toxins. For Sharon, high blood sugar was a toxin. To help cleanse her body, she committed to drinking between 96 and 128 ounces of water every day. She made water a routine part of her daily life.

In the United States, water is abundant in most states and territories. Nearly every home has access to clean, safe drinking water straight from the tap. Take advantage of it and drink it. Water is one of the most essential elements of life. It was provided for all living things, including animals and plants. It is found in almost every food we eat and every beverage we drink. Given its importance, water should be a key part of restoring balance to the body's chemistry. In addition to supporting overall health, water plays a vital role in maintaining blood circulation and helping the kidneys filter waste from the body. Staying hydrated is one of the simplest and most effective ways to support your health.

My wife and I often hear the same arguments: "I do not like drinking water." "I do not want to keep running to the bathroom." "I am too busy at work to drink water." "I am in school all day and do not have easy access to water." These are all excuses, no different from saying something as unrelated as, "My cat has diarrhea, and the house is a mess." If you truly want to heal your body and maintain good health, drinking water is essential. Make it a priority.

I see people carrying water bottles everywhere throughout the day. Some use commercial bottled water, similar to soda, almost as if it is a status symbol. Most of these bottles hold at least 16 ounces. Without even thinking about it, people often go through two or three bottles a day while at work or shopping. At the gym where my wife exercises, nearly everyone has a 16-ounce water bottle that they drink and finish during their workout. That alone adds up to three or four bottles, which is close to the recommended daily intake for a healthy person. If you also drink a glass of water with each meal and another with your medications, your daily intake reaches 80 to 106 ounces. Adding a glass of water during two snack breaks brings the total to 96 to 128 ounces, all without much effort.

Sharon fills a 32-ounce glass with water at least three times a day. She sips on it throughout the day, including during meals and snacks. When she goes to the gym, she takes a 32-ounce bottle of water and finishes it before returning home. Drinking four 32-ounce servings adds up to 128 ounces, which is equal to one gallon or two 2-liter bottles of water. This does not even include the occasional refill from the tap when she feels thirsty. So, what is your excuse?

Another common excuse for not drinking water is the preference for ice-cold water. Some people say they will only drink water if it is ice-cold. Sharon struggles with this. She finds that she can only take a few sips before it becomes uncomfortable for her stomach and body. While she can tolerate it better in hot weather, she still cannot drink it quickly or in large amounts. For her, room-temperature water is the easiest to drink and satisfies her thirst more effectively. I have even seen her drink nearly 16 ounces of water while taking her medication without any trouble.

Consider this. Your body temperature is 98.6 degrees Fahrenheit, while ice-cold water is around 40 degrees or lower. Room-temperature water is still cool at 70 degrees Fahrenheit. Your body only needs to warm it slightly before absorbing it into your tissues. When you drink room-temperature water, your throat does not tighten, and you do not experience chills. This makes it easier and more comfortable to drink. It works well for Sharon. However, if you prefer cold water, you can use an insulated water bottle to keep it at your desired temperature.

This strategy may not be exactly what you prefer, but give it a try and see if you can get used to it. Water plays an important role in metabolism. It helps break down food, reduces appetite, and can replace more expensive beverages. Most importantly, it helps the body eliminate toxins, including excess sugar. Keep in mind that what goes into your body must also come out. Be sure to plan for restroom breaks throughout the day.

I believe that if patients with kidney failure had been able to drink more water before their condition developed, they would have done so to prevent dehydration from damaging their kidneys. Similarly, if people had known that drinking more water could help reduce the effects of excess sodium on the body, they might have taken action before heart disease affected their health. This does not mean that water can cure chronic diseases. However, removing or diluting toxins in the body can help maintain overall health for as long as possible.

Drinking water is easy and highly beneficial for your body. When my wife does not drink enough, she actually starts to crave it. Since water has little to no taste, there is no reason to dislike it. What are you waiting for? Are you going to wait until you become sick, or will you take steps to stay healthy or regain your health? If you sweat excessively or engage in intense physical activity, you may need water with electrolytes, as long as it is sugar-free. However, plain water is still essential. This means not replacing it with coffee, beer, tea, soda, or juice. As Samuel Coleridge wrote in *Rime of the Ancient Mariner*, "Water, water, everywhere." The difference is that today, there is plenty to drink. So drink up, America. Stay healthy.

*Step Three*

# MEDICATIONS

Take your medications as prescribed. They are given for a reason and can save your life. For Sharon, medications played a key role in lowering her blood sugar along with other strategies. Your doctor will determine the medications that are best for you. Prescription medications are more effective than over-the-counter options, which may only be helpful for those with borderline diabetes.

It is important to inform your doctor about all the medications you are taking, including over-the-counter drugs and vitamins. Some vitamins and supplements, if taken at the wrong time, can interfere with the absorption of your diabetes medication. Your doctor needs a complete picture of your treatment to ensure it is safe and effective. Do not take unnecessary risks with your health.

Sharon took her medications to extend her life and protect her vision. Lowering her blood sugar quickly helped preserve her eyesight. She discovered that her high blood sugar had already caused slight damage to her eyes, particularly her retina. She also had high corneal pressure, which needed to be reduced to prevent further harm. Unlike other parts of the body, the retina does not heal. Once it is damaged, the effects are permanent. Sharon's top priority was, and still is, to protect her vision for as long as possible. She understood that the only way to achieve this was by bringing her blood sugar down to normal levels as quickly as possible. She also committed to following her eye doctor's strict monitoring and glaucoma prevention program. This extra care might not have been necessary if she had not developed diabetes, but she made it a priority to safeguard her vision.

Part of managing diabetes includes attending diabetes management training. My wife completed this training and also participated in follow-up sessions. During the training, several important topics were covered. Participants learned how to take blood sugar readings. There was also a brief discussion on blood sugar control medications, including insulin. However, this topic was not explained in detail, at least not to my wife's satisfaction. The training also provided guidance on reading and understanding nutrition labels on packaged foods. Participants learned how to track total carbohydrates per meal, per snack, and per day. Foot care was another important topic covered in the sessions. Since the diabetes management class lasted only two days, it was not possible to go into depth on every subject. My wife believes that at least five days of training would be necessary to fully understand these topics. This education is just as important as taking medications and following other health strategies because it provides a basic understanding of how to manage diabetes effectively.

*Step Four*

# EXERCISE

Sharon realized that she needed to burn the carbohydrates in her body. However, because she was overweight, she could not manage long hours of exercise. She also lacked proper exercise equipment at home and felt that the distractions in the house made it difficult to stay motivated. Years ago, she had purchased a lifetime membership at a major gym, but it was not in our area. She decided to look for a gym nearby that would be more convenient. After researching costs and available programs, she found one that suited her needs. The gym she chose offers frequent group classes focused on cardio, weightlifting, and stress reduction. It has both morning and evening sessions, making it easier to fit exercise into her schedule. In addition to group classes, the gym provides treadmills, free weights, and various exercise machines. She found a clean and well-equipped gym close to our home that offers a variety of health programs, not just exercise. The membership fee is affordable at $25 per month, making it a practical choice for maintaining her fitness routine.

Sharon goes to the gym almost every day. In the beginning, she attended one or two morning classes and then returned in the evening for another class, spending up to three hours per day exercising.

Because she was overweight, she used the treadmill three times a week to help burn fat. She had to start slowly since she was not used to walking fast or covering long distances. In her weightlifting classes, she began with little or no weight and gradually increased to nearly average weights. Due to arthritis in her knees, she avoids lunges and squats. Instead, she focuses on leg-strengthening exercises that are easier on her joints.

Almost everyone at the gym knows or recognizes Sharon. She is a regular member. She no longer spends several hours there each day. Instead, she attends one or two classes on most days, usually four to six days a week. During her first six months, she did not lose any weight. However, she saw a significant drop in her blood sugar levels. Within a month of starting regular exercise, her blood sugar decreased from 465 to the mid-100s. This was a great improvement, but she was determined to lower it even further.

Before this, Sharon rarely left the house except for errands. She struggles with an anxiety disorder, which makes her hesitant to go out. However, because protecting her vision is so important to her, she made the decision to leave home and exercise regularly. Exercise provides many benefits beyond lowering blood sugar. It strengthens the heart, reduces blood pressure, and improves overall mood. However, these benefits only come from taking action. Thinking about exercise is not enough. You must commit to doing it.

Life is full of compromises. Work, family, PTA meetings, garden club, hobbies, and many other activities can fill your day. However, making time for exercise is essential. You should aim to exercise almost every day for at least one full hour. This commitment must come from everyone, including yourself. Sharon struggled to find the time for exercise, and I also had to support her by making sure she could prioritize it. Taking time to preserve her vision and protect her health is far more important than any daily routine.

Fortunately, she did not have to give up much television time. Our satellite receiver includes a digital video recorder, which allows us to record the shows we truly want to watch and view them at our convenience. Our television also has a feature that lets us rewind up to one hour, making it easy to catch up on anything we miss.

Sharon had to step out of her comfort zone and become less reclusive in order to exercise and protect her eyesight. This was her major trade-off. Exercise also gives her the flexibility to have a snack, but not an entire meal made up of snacks. If she does not exercise, she sometimes chooses to skip her snack because she has not burned the calories or does not feel she has earned the extra carbohydrates. However, there are times when she must have a snack, regardless of whether she exercises. If her blood sugar drops too low, she may feel dizzy or confused, making it necessary to eat something immediately. Diabetics need to keep their carbohydrate levels within a healthy range. This means they cannot skip meals, and snacks must be planned in advance to maintain stable blood sugar levels.

Family and children are often the biggest reasons people give for not exercising. If you were undergoing chemotherapy or dialysis, your family would understand the need to prioritize your health. However, because high blood sugar does not always cause immediate or visible symptoms, both you and your family may overlook its seriousness and make other demands on your time. It is important to remember that high blood sugar can lead to severe, life-threatening complications. Managing it must be a daily priority. You must stay committed to keeping it under control every single day.

Your children do not stop seeing their friends. You make sure they do their homework so they can succeed in school and build a good future. In the same way, exercise is your homework. Your health is just as important as their education. Children can complete their homework on their own, and they can also learn to take on more responsibilities around the house. You must prioritize your health and commit to staying well. Just as you would make time for your children to take their medicine when they are sick, you must make time for exercise because it is your medicine. I have noticed that when Sharon misses several days of exercise, her physical health declines—she experiences dizziness—and her mental outlook worsens.

Sharon exercises four to six times a week. However, there are times when she is sick or overwhelmed with errands and exercises less. If she is too ill, she does not go to the gym, though this rarely happens. In times of serious family emergencies, she also has to reduce her exercise routine.

I understand that if she does not exercise regularly, her health may decline, and she could lose her sight. Despite her own challenges, she helped me during my recovery. She lifted me out of bed and into a wheelchair by herself until I was strong enough to do it on my own. Even with these responsibilities, she still made time to exercise. There were times when I had to wait for her, but I now have peace of mind knowing that Sharon is protecting her eyesight and her health, ensuring she will be with me for many years to come.

Life will always present challenges. However, if my wife continues to exercise regularly, missing a few days each month will not have a significant impact on her overall well-being. Her body will adjust, and occasional breaks will not undo her progress. As a result, I will have a wife who can continue to see and, hopefully, avoid the need for kidney dialysis. There are no guarantees, but she is doing everything possible to protect her vision and improve her health. I fully support her efforts, just as she supports me in my journey to better health.

*Step Five*

# DIET MANAGEMENT

Weight control and food management are the next major concerns. While losing weight can be beneficial, it is not the most important factor in managing diabetes. Many diabetics are thin, proving that weight alone is not the issue. However, for someone who is overweight and struggles with food, like my wife, weight loss should be a priority. For her, food is more than just nourishment—it is an addiction. Just as alcohol is the drug of choice for alcoholics, food is the substance that some people rely on in an unhealthy way. Unlike drugs or alcohol, food is legal and necessary for survival, making it even harder to control. Those who struggle with overeating often do not know when to stop, nor do they want to. They eat simply because food is available and enjoyable. Overeating is not just about satisfying hunger; it is often about seeking comfort. Eating brings emotional relief, leading to excessive food consumption. Many who struggle with food addiction prefer large portions and frequently eat multiple servings in one sitting—not just to satisfy a craving, but to prolong the pleasure of eating.

> **CAUTION!**
> **SUGAR FREE DOES NOT MEAN LOW CALORIE**

Food is made up of three main components: protein (5 calories per gram), carbohydrates (5 calories per gram), and fats, also known as lipids (9 calories per gram). Water and minerals are also present in food but are not the focus here. Proteins are essential for building muscles and producing enzymes that support vital functions in the body. Carbohydrates serve as the body's primary source of energy. They are not limited to sugars like sucrose and glucose; they also include starches and certain alcohols. In addition, carbohydrates and fats can combine with proteins to help form body structures. Fats act as the body's energy reserves and enhance the flavors in food. Most foods contain a mixture of protein, carbohydrates, and fats. Maintaining a proper balance between these three components is essential for good health.

It would be easier to manage our diet if foods contained only one type of nutrient—protein, carbohydrates, or fat. This would allow us to monitor exactly what we consume. However, the body requires balance. Too much protein can strain the kidneys, excessive fat can damage the circulatory system, and too much sugar can overwork the pancreas, which is especially dangerous for diabetics. My wife loved sugar—not just in donuts and candy, but also in bread, pasta, and other carbohydrate-rich foods. She enjoyed breaded fried chicken and rice. She liked vegetables, fruits, and juices. In short, my wife was not only addicted to food but also highly dependent on carbohydrates.

She had to adopt a sustainable diet that controlled her carbohydrate intake—enough to fuel her body but not so much that it worsened her diabetes. She also had to regulate her protein consumption to protect her kidneys and limit her fat intake to keep her heart and circulatory system healthy. My wife had to educate herself about food and how it affects her body.

A high-protein and high-fat diet provides my wife with plenty of food options. It allows for easier control of her calorie intake while keeping her carbohydrate levels in check. Protein breaks down into usable fuel for the body, and fat also converts into energy. However, relying solely on protein and fat is not a balanced or healthy approach. Our Creator designed our bodies to process carbohydrates as well. My wife had to learn how to choose the right carbohydrates and identify which types are best for managing her condition.

A single serving of carbohydrates (carb serving) equals 15 grams. According to the hospital dietitian, women are allowed three carb servings per meal, while men are allowed four. My wife often complains that it is unfair for men to receive more servings than women. I remind her that life is not always fair. Diabetics are also advised to have a morning and afternoon snack, each consisting of one carb serving, to help maintain stable blood sugar levels.

My wife read pamphlets and literature on diabetes to learn more about food choices. She discovered that most vegetable serving sizes range from ½ cup to 1 cup per carbohydrate serving, depending on the type of vegetable. However, some vegetables are classified as free carbohydrates, meaning they do not need to be counted as part of her daily carbohydrate intake. Most free carbohydrates come from vegetables that grow close to the ground and are naturally cultivated in sunlight. Examples include celery, lettuce, broccoli, green peppers, radishes, and beans. These foods help her feel full without significantly impacting her blood sugar levels. While free carbohydrates may not be as sweet or flavorful as fruits like oranges, grapes, cherries, and watermelon, they are still satisfying and provide excellent sources of fiber. In general, fibrous vegetables fall into the category of free carbohydrates.

Tomatoes are another example. They are low in calories and can be enjoyed in many ways, including whole, in spaghetti sauce, or as salsa.

During her first three months, my wife decided to eliminate added sugar from her diet, specifically sucrose. She required nearly everything to be sugar-free. To sweeten her cereal and coffee, she used sugar substitutes. She and I were already accustomed to drinking diet soda. She stopped eating cakes, frosting, and donuts. However, she continued consuming bread and skim milk, which naturally contain sugar. Milk, for example, contains lactose, a type of sugar composed of one molecule of glucose and one molecule of galactose.

My wife researched pasta and rice because she loves both. However, what she discovered was disappointing. Both foods cause a sharp rise in blood sugar, just like sucrose. They are high in carbohydrates, and even whole-grain or brown pasta has the same effect as regular pasta. Fortunately, there are alternatives. One option is Dreamfields® pasta, which contains only 5 grams of digestible carbohydrates per serving, compared to 41 grams in traditional pasta. While it does not taste exactly the same, it is a lower-carb alternative. Another option is spaghetti squash. My wife tried it but did not enjoy the taste or texture, even with spaghetti sauce. However, some people do, so it may be a good substitute for those who like it. As for rice, my wife has yet to find a carbohydrate-friendly version that works for her. Because of this, she has completely removed rice from her diet.

Breads such as muffins, rolls, cereals, donuts, cakes, and loaf breads can be harmful to diabetics because they are high in carbohydrates. Wheat itself is a carbohydrate, and sugar is often added to enhance flavor and texture.

In addition, these baked goods typically contain high amounts of fat, which makes them moist and more flavorful. White loaf bread (sandwich bread) is especially high in carbohydrates (15 grams per slice) and calories (70–80 calories per slice). However, lower-carb options are available, with some loaf breads containing only 8 net grams of carbohydrates and 35 calories per slice while still tasting good. The term net carbohydrates refers to the total carbohydrates in a food minus its fiber content. For example, if a food has 20 grams of total carbohydrates and 5 grams of fiber, the net carbohydrates would be 15 grams, which counts as one carbohydrate serving.

Nuts and berries are generally good options for managing carbohydrates. However, if you have a nut allergy, you should avoid them, as well as any other foods that may trigger an allergic reaction. Nuts release carbohydrates slowly, making it easier for the body to regulate blood sugar levels. They can even help lower blood sugar. However, one drawback is their high calorie content—a 1-ounce serving (about a small handful) contains around 170 calories, which can make weight loss more challenging. Nuts are also high in fat, so portion control is important. Berries typically have fewer carbohydrates than most other fruits. A single serving is usually one to one and a half cups. They are delicious and rich in antioxidants. However, fresh berries can be more expensive than fruits like oranges and apples, which makes them less accessible for some people.

You can eat other fruits, but portion control is important. Apples are high in fiber, but their size matters. If you do not want to or cannot share an apple, you may eat the whole fruit. However, apples do not stay fresh for long, they turn brown and become soft. Despite this, they remain a good source of fiber. Oranges should be eaten in small portions, so you may need to share or save the rest for later. If you enjoy grapes, a single serving is limited to 15 grapes, the same amount as 15 raisins. It is essential to watch serving sizes carefully. Just because a food is fruit does not mean you can eat as much as you want. Fruit juice is generally not recommended because it is a concentrated form of fruit with little or no fiber. My wife finds that eating whole fruit is more satisfying than drinking 2 to 4 ounces of fruit juice, which counts as a carbohydrate serving. However, if you prefer juice, you may have it—just be sure to check portion sizes and review the nutritional information.

If you eat meat, including it in your diet can help control your appetite because meat takes longer to digest, keeping you full for a longer period. However, meat also contains fat, so it is best to choose leaner cuts. Higher-fat meats, such as bacon, can still be enjoyed occasionally but should be considered a special treat rather than a regular part of your diet.

If you do not eat meat, it is important to find other sources of complete protein to meet your body's needs. Whey protein is one option that can enrich your diet. Mixing whey protein with water can be a good alternative, but it does contain some carbohydrates. While this cannot be avoided, it helps curb hunger and supports balanced nutrition. Our bodies require essential amino acids that we cannot produce on our own. These amino acids, found in proteins, play a vital role in building enzymes and body structures. Maintaining balance in your diet is key to good health.

Fats and lipids (commonly referred to as fats) are often overlooked. While they are essential for health, they should be consumed in moderation. Fats play an important role in food by enhancing flavor and storing energy. They also contain steroids and hormones that the body needs. Some people distinguish between fats (solid at room temperature) and oils (liquid at room temperature), but both serve the same purpose in the body. The body stores fat as energy for future use when protein and carbohydrate reserves are depleted. Oils also contribute to healthy skin, shiny hair, and the formation of body structures when combined with proteins. To maintain a balanced diet, fat intake should be limited to less than 30 grams per day, with a preferred target of less than 25 grams. Prioritize healthy fats for better well-being!

My wife occasionally consumes sucrose, but she does so deliberately and in controlled amounts. She sometimes enjoys mini candy bars, each containing 5 grams of carbohydrates. On special occasions like birthdays or weddings, she allows herself a small piece of cake with frosting. However, she treats sugar as an occasional indulgence rather than a regular part of her diet. Twice a year, she temporarily sets aside her dietary restrictions and enjoys a day without counting sugar, calories, or carbohydrates. She rarely drinks alcohol, usually limiting herself to one or two drinks per year. Since being diagnosed with diabetes, I believe she has had only one glass of wine. Alcohol is high in sugar and carbohydrates, making it an unsuitable choice for her. Instead, she prefers fresh fruit, which satisfies her cravings without the additional risks associated with alcohol. Each person must find their own way to balance enjoyment and health. Life requires balance—make mindful choices that work for you.

Learning to eat healthily is essential for long-term well-being. My wife carefully monitors her calorie intake, making sure that most of her calories come from nutritious foods rather than empty carbohydrates and fats. However, she still allows herself some empty calories, but in much smaller amounts than before. On average, empty calories make up only 100 to 200 calories per day in her diet. It is not perfect, but it is a significant improvement. She has lost nearly 50 pounds and successfully maintained her weight loss. Although she is no longer actively losing weight, she has seen major health benefits from the changes in her diet. She can now walk without experiencing back spasms, something that was once a struggle. She also has arthritis in one knee, which was worsened by her previous weight. However, with the weight loss, her knee pain has significantly improved.

My wife will always have a weight problem because she has a strong attachment to food. She will always struggle with her weight. However, she has gone from a 3X size to a large, which is a significant improvement. So far, she has successfully maintained her weight. Exercise and caloric restriction help, but there is only so much she can do. Her blood pressure is generally 110 or lower over 70 or lower, which is within a healthy range. After being diagnosed with Type II diabetes, her cholesterol initially rose to just over 200. This occurred because she ate large amounts of meat and eggs to help control hunger but did not maintain a balanced diet. Now that she is taking a cholesterol-lowering medication and monitoring her food intake, her cholesterol level has dropped to 120 or lower. Her good cholesterol is within the normal range. Her doctor has also tested her liver and kidney function, both of which remain well within the normal range. After three years, her A1C is now 5.4, a significant achievement.

# TYPICAL DAILY DIET FOR MY WIFE

| BREAKFAST |
|---|
| - A bowl of cereal (2 carb servings)<br>- 2-3 oz. skim milk (½ carb serving)<br>- 1 piece of toast with margarine and no-sugar-added jelly (½ carb serving)<br>- 16 oz. of water<br>- Coffee with a sugar substitute |
| **MORNING SNACK** |
| - An apple (1 carb serving)<br>- 16 oz. of water<br>- Coffee with a sugar substitute |
| **LUNCH** |
| - A sandwich made with low-carbohydrate bread, one slice of cheese, one slice of luncheon meat, and 2 teaspoons of low-fat/low-calorie spread or mustard (1 carb serving)<br>- A 100-calorie bag of chips or dessert (1 carb serving)<br>- 16 oz. of water<br>- A 12 oz. diet soda |
| **AFTERNOON SNACK** |
| - A protein bar (1½ carb servings)<br>- 16 oz. of water |
| **DINNER** |
| - 6 oz. of meat<br>- A free-carbohydrate vegetable<br>- A serving of a starchy vegetable (1 carb serving)<br>- 16 oz. of water<br>- A large bowl of berries with low-calorie whipped topping (1½ carb servings)<br>- A 12 oz. diet soda |
| **AFTER-DINNER CRAVING** |
| - A bowl of sugar-free Jell-O with low-calorie whipped topping (50 calories, no carbohydrates) |

TYPICAL DAILY DIET FOR MY WIFE

*Step Six*

# ADEQUATE SLEEP

Diabetics, like everyone else, require adequate sleep. In my wife's case, this means six to eight hours of sleep per night. Each person has their own sleep requirement. Getting the required sleep helps my wife manage her diabetes. When she gets enough rest, she does not feel as dizzy (which often happens when she lacks sleep) and does not feel as hungry.

When my wife does not get enough sleep, her morning blood sugar, which is normally between 100 and 110, fluctuates—either higher or lower. If it is higher, it usually rises to between 115 and 140. If it is lower, it drops to between 60 and 80, which explains her dizziness. In either case, lack of sleep disrupts her diabetes management and increases her appetite throughout the day.

Sleep helps to heal the body. Sleep reduces bodily stress. Sleep is a requirement for the body and a necessity that assists in keeping my wife's morning fasting blood sugar between 100 and 110.

# SUMMARY

### STEP ONE: SET YOUR PRIORITIES

To take control of your life and manage your diabetes effectively, setting priorities is essential. You need a strong reason to stay committed to controlling your diabetes. For example, my wife's reason is to protect her eyesight and maintain a good quality of life in her old age. When prioritizing your time, consider essential factors such as hydration, proper medical care, exercise, healthy food choices, and adequate sleep.

### STEP TWO: STAY HYDRATED

Drinking enough water (64 oz to 128 oz per day) helps regulate blood sugar levels and supports diabetes management.

## STEP THREE: SEEK PROPER MEDICAL CARE

Regular medical check-ups, health monitoring, early diagnosis, and appropriate medications are crucial for managing diabetes effectively.

## STEP FOUR: EXERCISE REGULARLY

Exercise not only helps control diabetes but also improves overall health. Maintaining a balanced lifestyle is essential. To keep your body functioning well, you must stay active and ensure that your body chemistry remains stable.

## STEP FIVE: FOLLOW A HEALTHY DIET

Diet plays the most critical role in diabetes management. Sugar (carbohydrates) is harmful to diabetics. Consuming too much sugar damages the body over time. It may not be as immediate as a bullet, but it gradually weakens and deteriorates the body.

## STEP SIX: GET ENOUGH SLEEP

Adequate sleep supports diabetes management, reduces stress, and improves overall health. It also helps prevent other illnesses and promotes general well-being.

# CONCLUSION

There are 25 million (and rising) diagnosed diabetics in the United States, with many being Type II diabetics. Additionally, an estimated 5 to 10 million people in the U.S. have undiagnosed Type II diabetes. This means that nearly one in ten Americans is diabetic and must carefully manage sugar and carbohydrate intake. It is also estimated that one-third of the American population is obese. While not all obese individuals develop diabetes, obesity significantly increases the risk of becoming diabetic.

This should serve as a wake-up call. Diet and exercise must become a more significant part of American life. Schools and businesses should promote, or even require, time for physical activity. Physical education and active recess should be mandatory in school curriculums. Health insurance should contribute to gym memberships as part of a proactive health prevention program, potentially saving millions of dollars in future healthcare costs. People should prioritize exercise in daily life. Instead of competing for parking spaces closest to a building, they should opt for spots farther away to encourage more walking. If one needs to go up four or fewer storeys in a building and is physically able, they should take the stairs instead of the elevator. Walking more and incorporating physical activity into everyday routines can reduce the need for separate exercise time. However, achieving a healthier lifestyle often requires balance and compromise.

Eating habits among all Americans should change. While vegetables, fruit, bread, cake, pasta, pizza, and candy are enjoyable to eat, not all carbohydrates are beneficial to the body. The pancreas regulates blood sugar levels, but it has its limits. Over a lifetime, the pancreas can only process a certain amount of sugar in the blood before its function weakens.

Parents must recognize that high-sugar diets may not be healthy for them or their children. This includes fruit juices, which contain high amounts of sugar. Instead, drinking water, eating whole fruits, exercising, and getting sufficient rest contribute to better health.

Life requires balance, and people should strive to achieve it. My wife has made healthier compromises to improve her well-being. As a result, her blood chemistry has significantly improved. Many of us talk about making healthier choices, but now is the time to take action.

Due to the changes in my wife's eating habits and lifestyle, I have improved my own ability to balance my life. I carefully monitor my diet, considering both calorie and carbohydrate intake. Although I am obese, I do not have high blood sugar, high cholesterol, or high blood pressure. However, I am at a higher risk of developing these conditions. I have personally lost 180 pounds. It has not been easy, but I remain committed to making healthier choices.

American food manufacturers can take steps to lower the carbohydrate and calorie content of foods. Cake mixes can be made with less sugar, and canned cake frostings should have sugar-free or no-sugar-added options. Foods can also contain higher amounts of both soluble and insoluble fiber. Breads can be both flavorful and lower in carbohydrates and sugar. However, it is important to remember that foods like cakes should be considered a "special" treat and not consumed daily.

Each of us must learn to make healthier choices in both our diet and lifestyle. If we do not, the day may come when more than 50 percent of the American population has diabetes. Conversations about A1C levels will become common, and many will rely on diabetic medications. A significant number of people may experience blindness, require kidney dialysis, or face limb amputations due to diabetes-related complications.

My wife has made great progress in managing her diabetes. She was diagnosed in her early 50s, which I find far too young. We all need to be more mindful of what we eat and make time for regular exercise. It is crucial to educate ourselves about diabetes prevention and take better care of our health. By doing so, we may help delay the onset of Type II diabetes, making it a condition that develops at 80 or 90 years old rather than at 50 or younger.

My wife made unhealthy choices earlier in her life. Now, she makes better decisions to protect her eyesight and improve her quality of life as she ages. She has successfully managed her diabetes and continues to do so.

I am sharing the six-step approach my wife followed to take control of her health and successfully manage her diabetes. Her goal is to ensure that diabetes does not defeat her. Will it defeat you?

# ABOUT THE AUTHOR

Dr. Johnson holds a Doctorate and a bachelor's degree in engineering, along with a master's degree in program management. He is a highly recognized researcher, tester, evaluator, and developer with 40 years of experience. He has documented his observations on how his wife managed to save her life after being diagnosed with diabetes.

www.ingramcontent.com/pod-product-compliance
Lightning Source LLC
Chambersburg PA
CBHW060858050426
42453CB00008B/1020